in the country garden
/
the end of england

Jack Young

SPAM Press
Glasgow 2023

What follows will bring about the end of the
idea of the isle that is known as England.

This poem shall cultivate a
grammar of weeds to open out its country
gardens into fields and meadows,
fens and woods.

I hereby summon the knights of Thomas
Malory's Morte D'Arthur to unravel the
nation that has for centuries been built upon
an overwrought dream/lie of civility, decorum
and moral fortitude.

Here, at the end of England, the knights &
plants & words doth revel in excessive delight
&
borderless horizons.

And vpon newe yeersday the barons lete maake a Iustes
and a tournement / that alle kny3tes shat wold Iuste or
tourneye / there my3t playe / & all this was ordeyned
for to kepe the lordes to gyders & the comyns / for the
Archebisshop trusted / that god wold make hym knowe that
shold wynne the swerd / So vpon newe yeresday whan the
seruyce was done / the barons rode vnto the feld / some
to Iuste / & som to torney / & so it happed that syre
Ector that had grete lyuelode aboute london rode vnto
the Iustes / & with hym rode syr kaynus his sone & yong
Arthur that was hys nourisshed broder / & syr kay was
made kny3t at al halowmas afore So as they rode to ye
Iustes ward / sir kay lost his swerd for he had lefte
it at his faders lodgyng / & so he prayd yong Arthur for
to ryde for his swerd / I wyll wel said Arthur / & rode
fast after ye swerd / & whan he cam home / the lady &
al were out to see the Ioustyng / thenne was Arthur wroth
& saide to hym self / I will ryde to the chircheyard /
& take the swerd that stycketh in the stone / for my
broder sir kay shal not be without a swerd this day /
so whan he cam to the chircheyard sir Arthur ali3t &
tayed his hors to the style / & so he wente to the tent
/ & found no kny3tes there/ for they were atte Iustyng
& so he handled the swerd by the handels / and li3tly &
fiersly pulled it out of the stone / & took his hors &
rode his way vntyll he came to his broder sir kay / &
delyuerd hym the swerd / & as sone as sir kay saw the
swerd he wist wel it was the swerd of the stone / & so
he rode to his fader Ector / & said / sire / loo here
is the swerd of the stone / wherfor I must be kyng of
thys land / when syre Ector beheld the swerd / he
retorned ageyne & cam to the chirche / & there they
ali3te al thre / & wente in to the chirche / And anon
he made sir kay swere vpon a book / how he came to that
swerd / Syr said sir kay by my broder Arthur for he
brought it to me / how gate ye this swerd said Ector to
Arthur / sir I will telle you when I cam for my broders
swerd / I fond no body at home to delyuer me his swerd
And so I thought my broder syr kay shold not be swerdles
& so I cam hyder egerly & pulled it out of the stone
withoute ony payn / found ye ony kny3tes about this swerd
seid sir ector Nay said Arthur / Now said Ector to Arthur
I vnderstãde ye must be kynge of this land :>>>>>>//////

i.

in the country garden hemmed in by walls i enact
my best thomas malory in my best bastard
prose/like malory i am searching for a new
language searching for new forms but i am sick
and rot-ridden over his england or anyone else's
england/i channel my inner-malory for his gay
and erring knights and his sentences that refuse to

*Well
/said
the
haut
prince
/this
day
must
noble
knights
joust*

Fig 044

Fig 044: References in middle english all come from Thomas
Malory's <Le Morte d'Arthur> which you can find online for
free here:

<https://quod.lib.umich.edu/c/cme/MaloryWks2/1:4.6?rgn=div2;view=toc>

<see <<Inventory>> section for QR scan>

i enact these words in a bid to find the end

in the walled country garden malory notes the roses climbing the daylilies luscious tongues extracted from native soil the foxglove spires dazzling purple loosestrife all frisky in the flowerbeds the irises vigorously bloom for queen and for country and

Fig h@4

Fig h@4: My sketch of the front cover of <Linnaeus: Organising Nature> by Liz Miles <Collins Big Cat/2017>. Carl Linnaeus was the 18th century Swedish botanist responsible for creating the Latinate taxonomy of plant classification still widely used today <or what could be called plant catalogue/ see <Inventory> section at the back>. This colonial taxonomy depicted species as pure and fixed biological forms/ with humans at the privileged centre. Any form falling outside these logical definitions was deemed monstrous :<any1 else fancy monsters?>:

<< a pause >>

<<<<<< archival interval 001 >>>>>>

country garden
country garden day nursery
country garden roses
country garden patio centre
country garden flowers
country garden ideas
country garden zoflora
country garden share price ─┐
country garden pottery
country garden soup

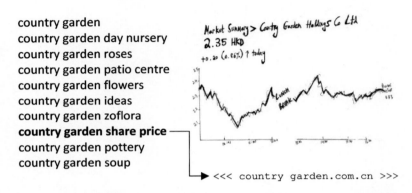

Market Summary > Country Garden Holdings Co Ltd
2.35 HKD
+0.20 (0.86%) ↑ today

    └─► <<< country garden.com.cn >>>

country garden holdings co ltd is a property development company in guangdong
china one hundred and fourty seventh in fortune global 500 hq in foshan number
of employees one hundred thousand and thirty nine two hundred and sixty
seven as of the year two thousand and twenty two the revenue was seventy
billion and thirty four million united states dollars the market summary on this
day is two point five hong kong dollars which is up zero point zero two zero and
a recent headline read

<<<chinas biggest property developer country garden sees
profits plunge 96%>>>

the company blames severe depression in the property market
and says that only the fittest will survive the fittest will
survive survival of the fittest in june 2017 country garden co
ltd halted all projects in china for security inspections
following an accident at its construction site in the eastern
province of anhui that killed six people survival of the
fittest only the fittest will survive in october 2018 country
garden co ltd via walker corporation was given approval to
develop stage one of south east wilton in sydney australia
controversial because the eastern side of the site will cut
koala corridors along allens creek only the fittest will
survive controversial because this area is home to the largest
recovering koala colony in new south wales survival of the
fittest only the fittest will

country garden
country garden day nursery
country garden roses
country garden patio centre
country garden flowers
country garden ideas
country garden zoflora
country garden share price
country garden pottery
country garden soup

<<< zoflora classic country garden concentrated multipurpose disinfectant >>>

take a breezy stroll through a country garden, blooming with delicate roses, English wildflowers and sweet blossoms in the fresh country air.

[please note: our orders are now fulfilled by our retail partner, Amazon]

<<< PRESS F1 FOR HELP >>>

Fig 0£f

The Weeds Act

1959 CHAPTER 54 7 and 8 Eliz 2

Fig 0££: << The Weeds Act 1959 >> was a piece of government legislation that attempted to <ctrl> what the government saw as <injurious weeds>/ therefore creating a distinction between <useful> and <not useful> plants </monsters?>. Some of the <weeds> listed were broad leaved dock/ creeping thistle/ ragwort and spear thistle.

Image:> Creative Commons author sodocan: <https://commons.wikimedia.org/wiki/file:Royal_Coat_of_Arms_of_the_United_Kingdom_(HM_Government,_1952-2022).svg>

ii.

a pause for the memory of plants taken from their soil/ do you not think/ do you not/ do you not notice how the plants have lost their capitals/ how the plants are losing their names in the garden and potions of hogweed mixed with oxlip and bladderwort and stinking goosefoot with scarlet pimpernel and round-leaved-sundew-redshank-rock-lettuce-red-tufted-vetch-ragwort-thistle-prickly-pear-leaved-cistus-meadow have stopped soothing the whirring white mind/ have stopped providing lethargy

the deadly

nightshade

o

ʻ

ͻ

ͻ

ᵱ   ꜱ

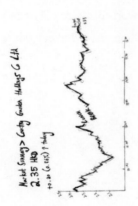

Market Summary > Garity Garden Holdings G LHA
2.35 HKD
+0.20 (6.665%) ↑ today

iii.

the deadly nightshade creeps as malory recedes and i give my body for a bean at the market where the exchange of pollen-cum-data-cum-money is worth more than the leaf-cum-precariat/ i know there is too little value prescribed no wait a minute for a second there and a minute and a second is time and time is money i thought i was saying the problem of prescribing value to the garden/ remember when every garden was a field/ do you remember/ remember when every garden was a field and really there was no need for a wall no distinction between inside and outside/ if we had our garden the horizon would be the border

If we had our garden the border would be the horizon

english plant
english plantain
english plants
english plant list
english plantain allergy
english plantations in Ireland
english plantation names in ireland

Fig MЄn7

<<< I've read the National Trust report and
it's a one-sided take on history/ full of
woke prejudices >>>

properties are named and shamed for their links to slavery
and colonialism as part of a nakedly political project

@daveangie167:
[replying to @nationaltrust]
what a load of pointless soul searching we cannot change history it happened get over it. What happens next is what is important

37   45

Fig M£n7: This headline references the 2020 National Trust report into their properties connections with slavery and colonialism/ which was met with widespread right-wing media backlash/ with charges that it was an attempt to <rewrite> english history

Fig UR3: Both memes are screenshots from the classic 90s arcade game <Commander Keen>/ a game I played as a kid and adored for its exciting/ other-worldy/ adventures/ and also the first time I ever encountered a computer. Was Commander Keen an Arthurian adventurer relocated to the 90s? Returning to this game as an adult/ I began to ask: what was the game saying about its white American hero/ and the terrifying aliens </monsters?> and landscapes he encountered?

You can play an online version of the game for free here and decide for yourself:
< https://www.playdosgames.com/online/commander/keen/4/ >

<see **<<Inventory>>** section for QR scan>

beyond the border i. fantasise about ripping petals to shreds/ leaving the stems exposed/ a different language of flowers a different kind of garden/ sometimes i fantasise about murdering petals/ morder in spanish tongue means to bite

WE MORDER THE PETALS !

Fig G£d

"And therefor, sir,' sende the Bysshop, 'leve thys opynyon, other ellis I shall curse you with booke, belle and candyll.''Do thou thy warste,' sende Mordred, 'and I defyghe the!

Fig G£d: My sketch inspired by page 11 of Aubrey Beardsley's 1893-4 illustrated version of <Le Morte d'Arthur>.

Beardsley was the most controversial artist of the Art Noveau era, renowned for dark and grotesque erotica. The queer coding in these illustrations really connects with my own interests in Malory/ finding something interesting in the way Arthur has been revisited during different eras to suit the dominant social projects of the time <in this context Victorian Imperial Britain/ with its strict moral code/ saw in Malory an emphasis on chivalry/ english exceptionalism and duty and honour>. Yet Beardsley/ part of Oscar Wildes countercultural sexually subversive circle/ was able to sneak into his illustrations the eroticism/ violence and instability beneath the surface of Malory's nation-building project of the late medieval period.

iv.

after morder the beech trees would shine all wild
and silvery in communal bee-glade bliss and
we'd make love hive-loud and dancing by the
moon/ somewhere we might be free/ stone
archways and walls would crumble in the acid-
joy of our rebellion and i would be jack-in-the-
green and green-fingered by love/ i would sense
your tulipped kisses thronging red in the
reddening sky and i know the sun is being
swallowed by the moon at the very same moment
that i am being swallowed by you/ we are spittle-
thick in the hawthorns at the edge of the garden/
at the edge of the field/ where many a deserter/
where many an errant soldier of brutal civil war/
hath unbuckled their breeches for freedom/ hath
breached the walls of england :>//////

And thus it   walls
past on   breach
from   walls breached
candylmas hath breached the
vntyl after hath breached the
ester that   walls
the moneth hath breached the
of may was   walls of england
come / whan   england walls
euery lusty   breached
herte   walls hath breached
begynneth   breached hath
to blosomme   hath walls
/ and to   wall
brynge   wa
forth   ha
fruyte /   h
for lyke as   a
herbes and   !
trees   ?
bryngen
forth
fruyte and
florysshen
in may / in
lyke wyse
euery lusty
herte that
is in ony
maner a
louer
spryngeth
and
florysseth
in lusty
dedes/

19

here in this field in england/ here on the edges of this field in england/ our backs turned on the lie that england always was/ the joke that just kept running/ in the garden beneath the walls/ in the market behind the freakshow/ in the curiosity cabinet beneath the museum/ in the factory next to the call centre/ in the industrial estate beside border control/ the joke that just kept running/ where I traded my body for a bean and found no beanstalk/ found no jack o the green dreams/ dreams just that/ distant and cloud-tipped and dissipating in mist/ the foot put in front of you guiding you no further in the field/ turning round in circles on the joke that was england that went on for far too long/ the mist of engl

and the idea of england/this rumour of
state and england/ oh england/ see our
crescent-mooned arses rise/ see them
eclipsing your long dusk at long last/
your sun is being swallowed at the edges
of the garden or field/ the names don't
matter anymore/ what matters is for a
moment i have my body back from the
market/ for a moment we are mandrake-
chested rebellion/ screaming from the
ground/ for a moment we are wandering
green-fronded with moonshining joy/ for
a moment we are bathing by the lambent
light of our raucous and waxy moon/
plum-ripe at the back-end of nowhere
and for a moment we have exposed
the whisper/ the rumour/ the crime

<< that was england >>

<< i enact these words in a bid to find the >>

a wonderful dreme

/

& that was this

/

that hym semed

/

he satte vpon a chaflet in a chayer

/

and the chayer was fast to a whele and therupon
satte kynge Arthur in the rychest clothe of gold
that myghte be made

/

and the kyng thoughte ther was vnder hym
fer from hym an hydous depe blak water

/

and there in were alle maner of serpentes and
wormes and wylde bestes foule and horryble

/

and sodenly the kynge thoughte the whele
torned vp soo doune

\

\

&

he

felle

amonge

the

serpentys

\

26

27

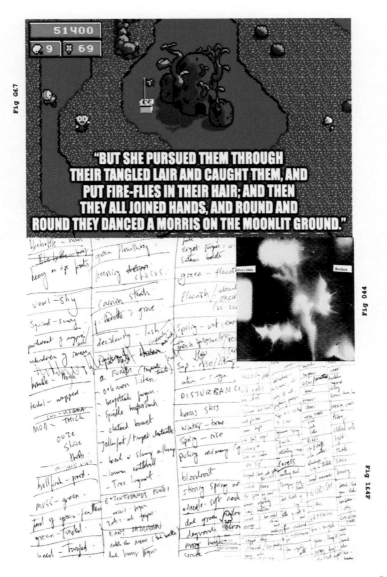

Fig GE7

"BUT SHE PURSUED THEM THROUGH THEIR TANGLED LAIR AND CAUGHT THEM, AND PUT FIRE-FLIES IN THEIR HAIR; AND THEN THEY ALL JOINED HANDS, AND ROUND AND ROUND THEY DANCED A MORRIS ON THE MOONLIT GROUND."

Fig 044

Fig 1E4F

28

Fig G£7: meme text is another classic retelling of medieval Arthurian myth: from Charlton Miner Lewis's <Gawayne and the Green Knight>. This was published around a decade later than Aubrey Beardsley's illustrated <Le Morte d'Arthur> in 1904.

You can find the full text online here:

<<<https://d.lib.rochester.edu/camelot/text/lewis-gawayne-and-the-green-knight>>>

Fig l£4F: plant and poetry notes are taken throughout from the back of my journal/ while scavenging across my neighbourhood.

<<< i enact these words in a bid to >>>

<<<<<< PRESS F1 FOR HELP >>>>>>

riotous spring	flurry – stews of the	broken – scratched	scattered coast line scallop with cover.
oil 4 Seette lava-flow	milky way.	honey suckle –sweet	
	thrush – nest worm.	OLD EVERANS	MOSS – green
		aurochs.	WOODS
tuss o clay field	becalmed – m.3 rivers, at calm @ all, prophesying paralysis	tarpans.	dandelion
		bison [fermented]	ragweed
wild garlic		boar	chicory
dog violets		beaver	Queen Annes
Sycamore bud-burst	the air clotted & slow.	deer.	keening cha
ribwal plantain.		MORE TREES birch oak Sallow.	thorny
yarrow bugle.	Sycamore –spinning.		riddled u light
birds foot trefoil.	Puck.	BIRDS chiffchaffs willow warblers bluebirds – sing in thickets	
cuckoo pint	ratcheting –wings		thrush.
lords and ladies			skein.
MO TE	**Caress**		
honeyed (thrush, pale -spotted stem - vile)	beetling dank.	wood anemones	keening
cuckoo flower .	thronging – dark streets.	EURISM.	beech – yew – 8
otter spoor by river.	dark thickets of ivory.	J.Mn.	hornbeam lively
broader upwelling.			
lady's bedstraw	nettle of root & seed.	GRYPHON	Decid Tr
sorrel bee orchid old rain bend	fern –shadowed.	fox – bright.	oak
borage			

Column 1 (left):

- bottle - bzz
- bottle - hum
- ~~Blue bottle - buzz~~
- my on ripe fruits

- owl - shy

- vole - scurvy

- scent of memory / ~~earth~~

- raven y sweep
- ~~...~~
- ...- thigh

- ...- wrapped

  SOIL - VISCERA
  THICK
      OOZE
      SLICE
      THROB
  BRUISED WOOD

- bullfinch - proud.

- MOSS - green.

- ...y green-feathers

Column 2 (middle):

- ragweed.
- Queen Anne's lace -
- green flourishing.
- evening ~~chorus~~ chorus.
- carrion stench.
- ii ~~...~~ > grave
- deciduously - lush
- ~~...~~
- a FUNGI (...)
  - oak moss lichen.
  - beefsteak fungus.
  - spindle toothbrush
  - clustered bonnet
  - yellowfoot / trumpet chanterelle
  - beech w shining milkcap.
  - common earthball
  - Tree lungwort.
- B. POISONOUS FUNGI
  - recoil - wgw
  - zombie - ...

Column 3 (right):

- POISONOUS FUNGI
- death cap
- fuse novel thru novel
- ergot fungus = WITCH TRIAL sit2ox?
- Satan's bolete
- green - flourishing
- flourish / abundance EXCESS.
  (vs. scarcity)
- Spring - wet, earth.
- fresh foliage... res, trans
- Sap - rise/rising.
- autumn - surge
- DISTURBANCE !!!
- humus shits
- Winter - brown.
- Spring - rise.
- pushing animary (of the woods
- bloodroot
- stirring spring woods
- needle - soft nook.
- dark green hemlock.

Inventory <INV>

>> Syr Thomas Malory <Le Morte d'Arthur> <William Caxton first edition/ 1485> Scan here to play:

>> Aubrey Beardsley's 1893-4 illustrations of <Le Morte d'Arthur> <Temple Classics>

>> Commander Keen/ game developed by id Software <1991>. Scan here to play:

>> Charlton Miner Lewis <Gawayne and the Green Knight> <1903>. Scan here to play:

>> the line <if we had our garden the horizon would be the border> is adapted from a journal entry by Derek Jarman in <Modern Nature> <Vintage / 2017>

>> Carl Linnaeus <Systema Naturae> <1736>

Inventory <N> <INV>

<early 15C>

>>from old french inventoire <detailed list of goods, a catalogue> <15c/ modern french inventaire>/ from medieval latin inventorium/ alteration of late latin inventarium <list of what is found> from latin inventus/ past participle of invenire <to find/ discover/ ascertain> <see invention>.

Note:>> this word emerges at a similar time to malory's <Le Morte d'Arthur> which is densely populated with french borrowings <see the title>/ following the norman conquest several centuries before.

<INV>

>> an abbreviation for inviting someone to join a multiplayer group/ used commonly in MMORPG games/ where players group together to accomplish objectives.

Interval \<INT\>

\<early 14C\>

\>\> \<time elapsed between two actions or events\> from old french intervalle \<interval/interim\> \<14c\>/ earlier entreval \<13c\> and directly from late latin intervallum \<a space between/ an interval of time/ a distance\> originally \<space between palisades or ramparts\> from inter \<between\> \<see inter-\> + vallum \<rampart/ palisade/ wall\> which is apparently a collective form of vallus \<stake\> from PIE \<walso- a post\>

Note:\>\> the end of england has brought down the rampart/ palisade/ wall\>

\>\> metaphoric sense of \<gap in time\> also was in latin from \<15c\> in english as \<a pause/ an interruption in a state or activity\> musical sense \<difference in pitch between two tones\> from \<17c\>

Note:\>\> a pause/ an interruption / / / / / /

acknowledgements

cover art:
untitled collage (2021)
sam williams
@s_a_m_w